NAVIGATING

Insights

THE WIT
& WISDOM
OF SKIP GRAY

FOREWORD BY JERRY WHITE

D1468773

Navigating Insights, copyright 2015, by Skip and Buzzie Gray.

ISBN 978-0-692-33804-9

Design: Steve Learned, ZignGuy.com

Cover Image: Klibbor, istockphoto.com

*Unless otherwise noted, Scripture taken from The Holy Bible, English Standard Version®
(ESV®) Copyright © 2001 by Crossway, a publishing ministry of Good News Publishers.
All rights reserved. Used with permission.*

Foreword

Truth is always wrapped up in words. When those words are put together in a way that makes us think, laugh, and remember, they stir up our minds and hearts to new ways of seeing God and life. For years my friend Skip Gray has blessed thousands of men and women with scriptural truth wrapped in quips and sayings that drive those teachings into their memory—and into their lives. Sometimes we get so serious that we miss the fun and humor that God naturally blessed us with.

What Skip writes is far beyond humor. Each quote has a context of a deeper message. The Preacher of Ecclesiastes says, "The words of the wise are like goads, their collected sayings like firmly embedded nails—given by one shepherd" (Ecclesiastes 12:11, NIV).

These sayings are meant to penetrate deeply into our minds and souls to help us think more clearly, to love God more fully, and to live our lives with commitment.

Skip has not only been a key and influential leader in The Navigators, but today he is sought after as a thoughtful and convicting speaker and teacher. Skip and with his wife, Buzzie, have deeply marked the lives of countless men and women. They have challenged people to live unswervingly for Jesus—and to do so with a wise balance of work, family, and activities in church and other ministries.

For many years Skip has ministered extensively in the community of medical doctors in particular, individuals whose lives are often pressed to the edge. As a result, he has helped them develop lives of passion for Christ and commitment to their families.

As you read and savor these rich statements, let them stir you to a deeper walk with Jesus.

Jerry White, Ph.D.
The Navigators International President Emeritus
Major General U.S. Air Force (Ret.)
January 2015

Introduction

Somewhere along the line of learning to communicate the precious truth of God's Word, two ideas surfaced that have proven to be helpful for me. Through the years there has been ample confirmation of their usefulness.

The first is "less is better." "One-liners" are more readily remembered than "long-liners." For example, "A sermon does not have to be eternal in order to be immortal."

The second helpful thought is that appropriate timely humor can facilitate the memory of the teaching in the mind and heart of the listener.

With these ideas in mind, the purpose of this little volume is twofold—to encourage your heart, and to enlarge your arsenal of verbal ammunition in order to better serve the Lord Jesus where you live, work, and play.

These insights surfaced in my many decades of ministry with the Christian organization called The Navigators. God has used these Navigating Insights to help me "navigate life spiritually." Again, I pray the "wit and wisdom" here will make a difference in your spiritual journey and personal ministry as well.

Finally, some of the thoughts are original. Others you may recognize having heard before and can testify to the wisdom of their authors. Toward the end I acknowledge the names of some of the authors who have deeply affected my life for good, and I share a few of their quotes for the sake of balance and perspective.

May these insights simply be a link in an unending chain of truth to set people free from the bondage of ideas that do not reflect God's love and grace toward each one of us.

Skip

Philip "Skip" Gray
January 2015

Contents

NAVIGATING

Insights

THE WIT
& WISDOM
OF SKIP GRAY

FOREWORD BY JERRY WHITE

Topics

Anger–Bitterness

Most anger is defending
your ego, your pride, and
your self-esteem.
Admit it, analyze it, and deal with it
(Ephesians 4:28).

What makes you angry is not
what someone else does to you but what you tell
yourself about what he or she has done.

Bitterness is a poison *you* swallow
and hope the *other* person dies.

Bitterness is an acid that destroys its own container.

Bitterness is the leading cause
of spiritual death in the church.

Bible

*A little bit of faith in
the promises of God is
more valid than a lot of faith
in anything else.*

The Bible without Jesus is unthinkable;
Jesus without the Bible is unknowable.

Truth in the Bible is in tension for the sake of balance.

Ask God for promises from His Word for you as a person,
a partner, a parent, and a professional.

God will be as specific with you as you are with Him.

In the temptation in the wilderness in Matthew 4
Jesus did not refer to His experience in Matthew 3,
"This is My beloved Son." He referred to God's Word
in Deuteronomy and submitted Himself to it.

You eat God's Word and it becomes the life of Jesus in you
(John 6:57-63).

Your spiritual immune system may be compromised
through spiritual malnutrition (Jeremiah 15:16).

There are no threats in the Bible. If I say,
"You're going to die," that's a threat. If God says,
"You're going to die," that's a promise.

Only two things in life are eternal: the Word of God
and the souls of people. Everything else is going to burn.
If mankind made it, God is going to burn it.

You may graduate from Bible school;
you never graduate from Bible study.

The Bible is the Sword of the Spirit (Ephesians 6).
A sword has two purposes—
hang it over the mantle or shed blood with it.

If there are ten people in a Bible study,
each person has nine instructors.

Sometimes we forget the promises we make.
God never forgets His promises.
Put all your weight on the promises of God.

The Bible is the exclusive validation of spiritual truth.

Every verse of Scripture has one valid interpretation;
it may have more than one valid application.

———————

We live in a moral universe created and governed by an
infinite, moral, personal God who has spoken.

———————

Christ in you is the sum total of
what you take in from His Word (2 Peter 1:3-4).

———————

When you read the Word look for:
- ► Commands to obey
- ► Examples to follow
- ► Errors to avoid
- ► Promises to claim
- ► Blessings to enjoy
- ► Questions to answer

———————

Your physical body (except for your brain,
the hard part of the femur, and a few other things)
is the sum total of all you have eaten the past 24 months.
You're just a "Big Mac" with a sweatshirt!
Your inner person is the sum total of all
you have eaten spiritually. Feed on Christ daily
(John 6:57,63 and Jeremiah 15:16).

Character

Reputation is
what we have during the day;
character is
what we have at night.

We are not for sale; we are bought with a price.

———

Most of us say, "I want patience and I want it right now!"

———

The bottom line of human experience
is the character of God.

———

God's rules for the kings of Israel from Deuteronomy
17:16,17—He shall not multiply gold, wives, or horses;
that is, don't get tripped up by money, sex, or power.

———

Every test you pass only qualifies you for a greater,
tougher test. For example, consider what happened
when Abraham left home (Genesis 12).
Then God asked him to sacrifice his son (Genesis 22).

———

Abraham, sacrifice your son (Genesis 22) …
and don't play with a rubber knife.

———

Satan whispers, "You are one of the few people who can get away with it."

———◆◆◆———

You can't carve rotten wood.

———◆◆◆———

Christian Life

Whenever God asks a question
it is not to gain information
but to help us
understand ourselves.

We are human beings not "human doings"; being is
ministry (2 Corinthians 3:18, 4:1); doing flows from being.

The safest place for a Christian is in combat
(remember David and Bathsheba).

Understand the difference between true guilt and false
guilt. True guilt (conviction of the Holy Spirit) is firm, gentle,
specific, and hopeful. False guilt (condemnation of the
devil) is harsh, vague, discouraging, and hopeless.

If you are a Philippians 4:13 person—
"I can do all things through him who strengthens me"—
you also need 2 Corinthians 13:4, "For he was
crucified in weakness, but lives by the power of God.
For we also are weak in him, but in dealing with you
we will live with him by the power of God."

If you're tempted to be discouraged, read Revelation 4
and 5—the final score is posted—we won!

In warfare being a casualty
is a matter of chance (wrong place at the wrong time).
In spiritual warfare being a casualty is a matter of choice.
There are no rubber bullets out there.

Luke 4 teaches us that when God leads you into
the wilderness, it's to settle the issue of your identity.
When He leads you into the synagogue,
it's to settle the issue of reputation.

Church

Jesus said, "You make disciples;
I will build my church,"
a clear division of labor.

A sermon does not need to be eternal
in order to be immortal.

———————

Often when church leaders meet to discuss
church business, they focus on six things:
bucks, buildings, bodies, buses, baptisms, and basketball;
rather than intimacy with Christ and
godly character based on biblical theology.

———————

You need the church more than the church needs you.
Loners don't make it.

———————

Your lifestyle is as important as your theology.

———————

Avoid Sunday morning "Billiard Ball Fellowship." Be real.

———————

The calling of the church staff is to teach, motivate,
delegate, and model (Ephesians 4:11-13).

———————

If you focus on leaders, you'll have growth. If you focus on growth, you'll have spiritually dead leaders.

———

It's the sheep, not the shepherd,
who give birth to the lambs.

———

You can tell whether churches are legalistic
or based on grace by whether they influence
by control or by relationships.

———

Some churches practice
"Committee thy way unto the Lord."

David's Example

How does God bring two men

together in mortal combat?

He uses a bag lunch.

We often miss God's opportunities

because we don't have time

for bag lunches.

When God is looking for a person to use in public,
He will find one He can trust in private.

———◆◆◆———

When a man is going to perform with two armies
watching, what counts is how he performs
with an audience of One.

———◆◆◆———

Don't go into battle with Saul's armor.

———◆◆◆———

Goliath could slam-dunk flat-footed. Saul said, "He's so big
he's going to kill us." David said, "He's so big I can't miss."

———◆◆◆———

God sees individuals, not masses. He looks at the heart.
Are you a person after His own heart (Acts 13:22)?

Discipleship

A person with a nail through his hands is not clinging to anything. Relinquish control.

You teach what you know. You reproduce what you are.

———————————

All it costs to invest in someone else is your life.
Isaiah 43:4, "I give men in return for you,
peoples in exchange for your life."

———————————

"If anyone would come after me, let him
deny himself and take up his cross daily and follow me"
(Luke 9:23). That's almost every day!

———————————

In Matthew 13:37-38, Jesus is the farmer, the field
is the world, the good seed are the children of the
Kingdom. God is planting you, His seed, in the world.
You are sinners, saints, sons, sheep, shepherds, soldiers,
servants and you are also seeds. Don't demand seeds'
rights; who knows best where to plant the seed?
A seed must lose its "selfness." It must disintegrate
and must die in order to bear fruit.

———————————

Salvation is free because it cost Jesus a cross.
Discipleship costs me a cross (Luke 9:23).

Faith

The original King-size bed

was a manger.

My view of I Peter 5:7, "Lord, I have the distinct impression that you have a serious problem."

Some people say, "faith without credit cards is dead."

Liberals have blown the war effort by denying the deity of Jesus. Evangelicals are blowing it by denying their own humanity.

Faith is only as valid as its object.

The just shall live by faith (Habakkuk 2:4, quoted three times in the New Testament).
1. Romans 1:17 – the JUST shall live by faith
2. Galatians 3:11 - The just shall LIVE by faith
3. Hebrews 10:38 – the just shall live by FAITH

Family

*When raising children,
remember more is caught
than taught.*

Relating to adult children:
Always claim the promises of God.

Never lose your sense of humor.

Rarely give unsolicited advice.

Forgiveness

*Forgiveness does not mean
it does not matter. At its root,
forgiveness is the choice
to pay the cost ourselves
rather than exact it from the
one who harmed us.*

I John 1:9 is the Christian's bar of soap.

Forgiveness is a life and death issue.

God's Will

*The will of God is an
eight-lane freeway,
not a tightrope
over Niagara Falls.*

The will of God is not a needle in a haystack.

———◆•◆———

90% of the will of God is asking the question,
"What do you enjoy?"

———◆•◆———

Need does not determine the will of God;
prayer does (Luke 5:15,16). Jesus left the unhealed
multitude and went to the mountain to pray.
Someone else's need does not automatically
become a demand on your resources.

Guidance

Don't play "Junior Holy Spirit."

90% of godly counsel is asking the right questions.

People who try to tell you what the will of God
is need a rowboat and a map to Niagara Falls.

Indecision is the key to flexibility.

"Mind reading" is not a gift of the Spirit.

Humility

The longer you walk with God

the more you understand

your need for humility.

Humility is the evidence of a person's value of God.
Integrity is the evidence of a person's value of self.
Sensitivity is the evidence of a person's value of others.

It spells **HIS**; summarized in Micah 6:8–
"He has shown you, O man, what is good and what does
the Lord require of you but to do justice (integrity), to love
mercy (sensitivity) and to walk humbly with God."

Humility is a man without pride;
Integrity is a man without price;
Sensitivity is a man without prejudice.

———◆◆◆———

John the Baptist said "He must increase,
but I must decrease"(John 3:30).

———◆◆◆———

Early in his ministry Paul said he was the
"least of the apostles" (1 Corinthians 15:9).
Later in his ministry Paul was the
"least of all the saints" (Ephesians 3:8).
At the end of his life Paul was
"the chief of sinners" (I Timothy 1:15 KJV).

———◆◆◆———

Satan exalted himself five times and God
cast him down from heaven (Isaiah 14:12-14).
Jesus stepped down, down, down five times and God
highly exalted Him (Philippians 2:6-11).

Humor

The difference between a drunk
and an alcoholic is
"Us drunks don't have to attend all
those meetings!"

God has a sense of humor; every Jewish man thanked
God daily that he was not a woman, a slave, or a Gentile.
In Acts 16, Paul's first converts were a woman,
a slave, and a Gentile!

Three things contribute to wellness:
prayer, good medicine, and humor.

The King James Version is
"Good News for 17th Century Man."

Empty garages and empty attics will
produce rational fanatics.

Jesus' Example

Jesus loved the world, helped many, and discipled twelve. He said, "As the Father has sent me, even so I am sending you" (John 20:21).

Jesus wanted radicals on His team. He chose the Twelve after they defied the system by picking grain on the Sabbath.

———◆◆◆———

There are only three things you can do in the life of another person: teach, pray, model— which is exactly what Jesus did.

———◆◆◆———

Jesus knew who He was (John 13:3). Only a person who knows who he or she is and is secure in Christ can love and serve as Christ did.

———◆◆◆———

Jesus is the "Three Mile an Hour" God. He did not go jogging through Judea, sprinting through Samaria, or galloping through Galilee. He walked slow enough that a hemorrhaging woman could touch Him and be healed.

———◆◆◆———

Jesus had two great works. In John 19, when He said "It is finished," He referred to Redemption.

In John 17, when He said "I have glorified You on the earth. I have finished the work which You have given Me to do" (NKJV). He referred to the Twelve.

Forty times in John 17, Jesus referred to *all* of the disciples God gave Him.

What are you going to say to God the night before you die? *I have finished the work You gave me to do!*

Life

*Avoid the
sacred/secular dichotomy.
All of life is sacred.*

"I have called you by name, you are mine" (Isaiah 43:1). The Lord wanted one just like you; two like you would be a disaster.

———

Your life purpose needs to be specific, measurable, and attainable. If you can't state your life purpose in 25 words or less, you don't have one.

———

Life is one big baggage claim area— not every suitcase has your name on it.

———

When in doubt throw it out.

———

When you're training a dog, you have to be smarter than the dog.

———

If you want to travel far, you must travel light.

———

I play golf in the spring, fish in the summer, hunt in the fall, ski in the winter, and preach in the off-season.

———

Every human institution has a shelf life.

———•••———

Worry works. Most of the
things we worry about never happen.

———•••———

It's difficult for a person to be the
center of the universe with limited resources.

———•••———

The Great American Pastime is not baseball, it's denial.

———•••———

You cannot live right if you believe wrong.
The only way to live right is to believe right. Your life is an
expression of what you believe deep down to be true.

Love

*God is too wise to do or allow
anything foolish; too loving
to do or allow anything unkind.*

The crown jewel of creation was a bride (Genesis 2).
The crown jewel of the new creation will be a bride
(Revelation 21:2,9). God has a thing about brides!

The opposite of love is not hate; it's indifference.
The essence of love is vulnerability.

God would rather you say "I hate you"
and mean it than "I love you" and lie about it.

Ministry

*There must be someone
who knows less about God than
you do. Find that person!*

Fishing for men is "catch and release."

———◆—◆◆—◆———

Ministry is relationship; leadership is influence.

———◆—◆◆—◆———

We are Ambassadors for Christ, not tourists.

———◆—◆◆—◆———

Some people are so busy they are skiing downhill
in front of an avalanche.

———◆—◆◆—◆———

A brief history of most human organizations: The Man, The
Mission, The Movement, The Monument, The Mausoleum.

———◆—◆◆—◆———

In a garden, the weeds always win.

———◆—◆◆—◆———

If you knew you were going to die tomorrow, how would
you spend your time tonight (email, texting, phone)?
Jesus spent it washing the disciples' feet.

———◆—◆◆—◆———

The only people you will minister to
are people who like you.

God is so desperate He'll even use you.

Obedience

In Philippians 4:8 Paul says,
"Think . . . "; in the next verse,
Philippians 4:9, he says,
"Do . . . " This is the Divine order.

If you are unwilling to do what God asks,
you're unqualified to do what you want.

———•◦•———

There are two kinds of Christians:
"Sea of Galilee Christians" who are alive and moving and
"Dead Sea Christians" who are stagnant.

———•◦•———

In college there are required courses and electives.
In God's training there are no electives.
He does not solicit our opinion concerning the curriculum.
He reserves the right to decide.

Relationships

When you are transparent
with someone, you open
your life to him or her.
When you are vulnerable,
you not only open your life
but also ask for his or her help.

When you hang out, good stuff happens (Acts 24:16).

———◦━◦◦━◦———

Be selective who cosigns your emotional checking account.

———◦━◦◦━◦———

What used to protect men from society was a drawbridge;
today it's a garage door opener or headphones.

———◦━◦◦━◦———

Who you associate with is as important
as what you believe.

———◦━◦◦━◦———

We impress at a distance. We impact up close.

———◦━◦◦━◦———

Dale Carnegie's second book was
How to Win Back Friends You've Influenced.

———◦━◦◦━◦———

In the Holy Land, Christianity was a relationship;
In Greece it became a philosophy; in Rome it became
an institution; in Europe it became a culture;
in America is has become an enterprise.

Salvation

When Jesus' heart stopped,
you were delivered from
the penalty of sin.
When Jesus' heart began beating
again, you were delivered
from the power of sin.
When your heart stops,
you will be delivered from
the presence of sin.

Pontius Pilate condemned the innocent and set free
the guilty. The next day God did the same thing.
He condemned Jesus and set us (the guilty) free.

Success

No one ever finished a race
accidentally. If you finish,
you finish intentionally. Jesus said
in John 17 that He finished God's
work because in John 4 He said
He planned to finish.
Paul said in 2 Timothy 4:7 that he
finished his race because in Acts
20 he said he planned to finish.

People learn more about the grace of God watching you handle failure (adversity) rather than success (prosperity).

"Waste time" profitably.

Trust

I have all the money
God can trust me with.

God will honor your stewardship
but challenge your ownership.

Christians don't worry; they're "concerned."

People only believe what they discover.

There are three levels of belief:
1. Opinion: fluid, changeable, "a dime a dozen"
2. Conviction: fewer, stronger, more thought through
3. Doctrine: normative for all believers in every culture or language

We don't impose our opinions or convictions on other people. But doctrine is what you die for.

Appendix

Wit and Wisdom from Other People

"The road to maturity must cross the
bridge of disillusionment."
—Richard Halverson

"The key to originality is to obscure the sources."
—Howard Hendricks

"Our peace will never come from an explanation;
it will come from a Presence."
—Billy Graham

"The future is as bright as the promises of God."
—LeRoy Eims

"The enemy of the best is not the poor but the good."
—Dawson Trotman

"When you're dealing with the devil,
never argue; always quote."
—Dawson Trotman

"God gave you a lot of guidance
when He gave you a brain."
—Dawson Trotman

"There are 2,600 people mentioned by name in the Bible.
Less than 100 finished well."

—Howard Hendricks

"I have never seen a hearse pulling a U-Haul trailer."

—Chuck Swindoll

"In the English language the word 'No'
is a complete sentence."

—Carole Mayhall

"Every religion in the world is advice.
Christianity is Good News."

—Timothy Keller

"God gives us what we would have asked for
if we knew everything that He knows."

—Timothy Keller

"Summary of the Bible:
Genesis 3 – Origin of Sin;
Romans 3 – Consequence of Sin;
John 3 – Solution for Sin."

—Jim Downing

"The Bible was not given to increase our knowledge
but to change our lives."

—D. L. Moody

About the Author

Philip "Skip" Gray has served with The Navigators for six decades. His primary focus is among physicians, both in his home state of Colorado and across the United States. He began ministering to physicians part time in 1975, seeking to help them with their spiritual lives, marriages and families, priorities and schedules, and ministries.

Since 1988 he has devoted the majority of his time to this ministry through conferences, extended personal time, correspondence, and telephone calls. He and his wife, "Buzzie," also minister to other professional groups, churches, and mission agencies in the United States and overseas.

Skip first learned about The Navigators while a student at Wheaton College in Illinois. He holds a degree in Christian Education and was ordained by the First Baptist Church of Wheaton. He has represented The Navigators since 1953 in Texas, California, Oregon, Georgia, South Carolina, and Virginia. He has also been "on loan" to the Billy Graham Evangelistic Association, Cru (formerly Campus Crusade for Christ), Pocket Testament League, Youth for Christ, and The Latin America Mission. The Grays served one term as missionaries in Costa Rica and minister on occasion in Spanish.

Skip and his wife Buzzie have three children. Ken is an attorney in Colorado Springs, where he lives with his wife, Debbie. They have five grown children. Dave is an engineer in Dallas, where Kathy and four boys complete his family. Daughter Carol Hatch is an oncology nurse in Denver, where she lives with her husband, Don, an aerospace engineer. Her four grown children are on their own. And the Grays enjoy numerous great-grandchildren.

Did you enjoy *Navigating Insights*?

Who else could be encouraged and inspired by the Wit & Wisdom of Skip Gray?

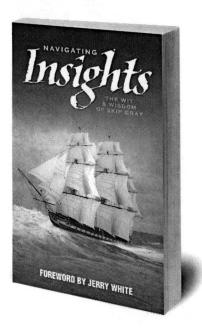

Order Additional Copies Today for:

- ► family & friends
- ► pastors & church leaders
- ► Bible studies & disciples
- ► colleagues & more

www.skipperpublishing.com

CPSIA information can be obtained
at www.ICGtesting.com
Printed in the USA
FSOW02n1045220416